Perfection Learning®

How Much Does It Weigh?

Cathy Elliott

1 ounce

The Post Office uses a **postal scale** to weigh mail. People buy stamps to pay for each ounce of weight. Most letters weigh up to one ounce.

Monkeys like to wiggle when they're weighed. Handlers use a **sling scale** to weigh a monkey. Adult spider monkeys weigh between 1 and 3 pounds.

1–3 pounds

7¹/₂ pounds

Doctors use a **baby scale**. The average weight of a new baby is 7¹/₂ pounds.

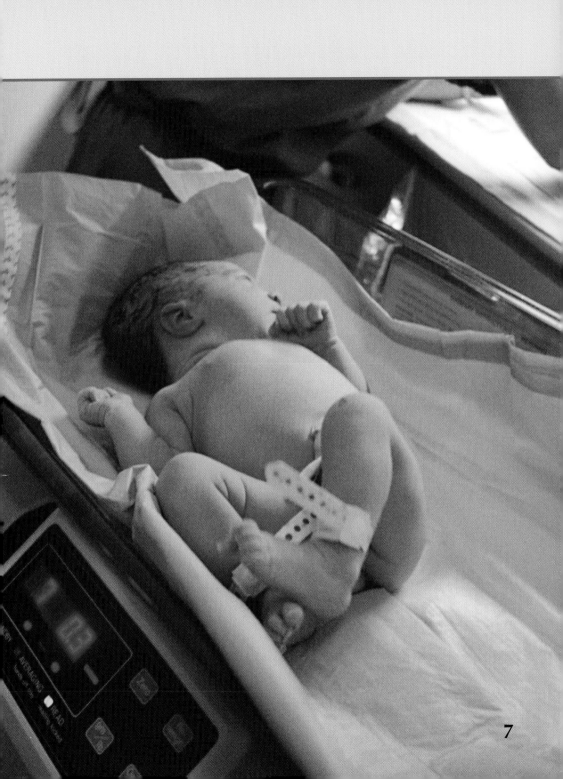

A **jockey scale** weighs both jockey and saddle. Most jockeys weigh around 112 pounds.

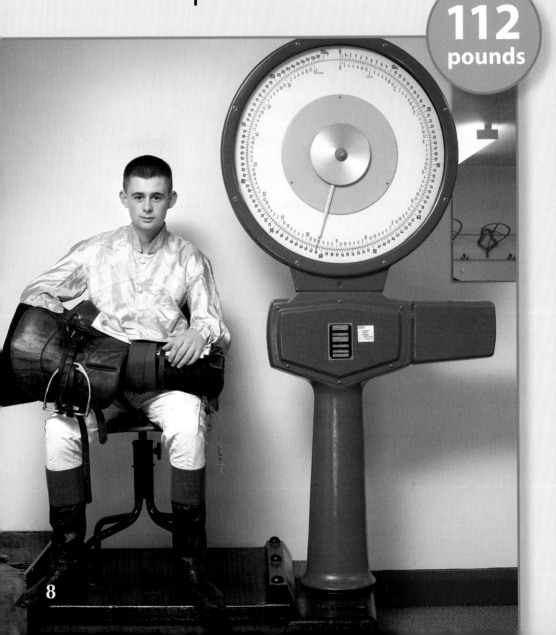

112 pounds

100–250
pounds

A **medical scale** is used to weigh people. Adult males and females usually weigh between 100 and 250 pounds.

9

It is hard to weigh a slippery seal.
Seals are weighed by a **marine scale**.
Male gray seals weigh between
375 and 880 pounds.

375–880
pounds

Ranchers need to weigh their cattle before they are sold. Cattle are weighed with **cattle scales**. An adult Angus cow may weigh as much as 1000 pounds.

80,000 pounds

A truck is weighed on a **truck scale**. A semitruck and trailer might weigh up to 80,000 pounds.

Glossary

Postal scale

Sling scale

Baby scale

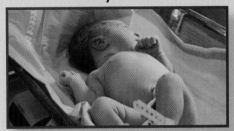

Jockey scale

Medical scale

Marine scale

Cattle scale

Truck scale

Reading Essentials®
Discovering Science

Leveled content-area science books in Earth/Space Science, Life Science, Math in Science, Physical Science, Science and Technology, and Science as Inquiry for emergent, early, and fluent readers

How Much Does It Weigh?
Written by Cathy Elliott

Text © 2006 by Perfection Learning® Corporation

For information, contact

Perfection Learning® Corporation

1000 North Second Avenue, P.O. Box 500
Logan, Iowa 51546-0500.
Phone: 1-800-831-4190
Fax: 1-800-543-2745

perfectionlearning.com

PB ISBN 0-7891-6731-x

1 2 3 4 5 6 BA 10 09 08 07 06 05

Image credits:

Cat Gwynn/CORBIS: p. 7; Chuck Haney: p. 13; David R. Frazier: p. 14; Frank Balthis: p. 10 (top); Getty (Rights-Managed): pp. 8, 10–11; Steve Kaufman/CORBIS: p. 5

Getty (Royalty-Free): p. 9; iStockphoto: pp. 4, 12, 15; Photos.com: cover, back cover, pp. 2, 6